Rookie
Read-About® Geography

Living Near
a River

By Allan Fowler

Consultant
Linda Cornwell, Coordinator of School Quality
and Professional Improvement
Indiana State Teachers Association

SCHOLASTIC INC.

New York Toronto London Auckland Sydney
Mexico City New Delhi Hong Kong Buenos Aires

ISBN   0-516-24175-3

12 11 10 9 8 7 6 5 4 3   5 6 7 8/0

Printed in the U.S.A.   61

First Scholastic printing, January 2003

Designer: Herman Adler Design Group

On maps, rivers are shown as thin, blue lines. Next to these blue lines are little circles or dots. They stand for towns and cities.

This map shows rivers, cities, and towns.

New York City and the Hudson River

Rivers flow past, or through, many of the biggest cities in the United States.

An example is New York City. It is on the Hudson River.

Long ago, people often settled next to rivers. They drank the fresh river water. They caught fish to eat.

A home built beside a river

This boat is taking people and goods down a river.

People used boats to travel on the rivers from place to place. They also used boats to ship goods.

Some cities arose as ports. A port is a town or city with a harbor where ships can dock.

There workers can load and unload goods.

Workers loading bags of sugar onto a ship

This ship is sailing down a river to enter the ocean.

Ports are usually located where a big river reaches the ocean.

Products from farms or factories or mines are carried to the port by ship.

From there, the goods are taken to other places by truck, train, or on another ship.

New Orleans, Louisiana, is a big port city. It sits where the Mississippi River meets the Gulf of Mexico.

The Mississippi River running through New Orleans

A city might also grow where two or more rivers come together.

Two rivers meet at Pittsburgh, Pennsylvania to form a third river.

Pittsburgh, Pennsylvania

There may be a waterfall or rapids along a river. That is as far as boats can go on a river. It is a good place to build a city or town.

A waterfall in Minneapolis, Minnesota

The force of water turns this waterwheel.

Many factories were built at such places. Falling or rushing river water turned waterwheels. Power to run factory machines came from the waterwheels.

Today, many people use dams to provide power called electricity.

This dam was built across a river to bring electricity to the people who live and work nearby.

This ditch holds water that is used for the fruit trees
planted on this California farm.

Food crops need water and moist soil. So people dig ditches and build pipelines. These carry the river water to their farms. This is called irrigation (ihr-uh-GAY-shun).

Some people live in areas where the land is dry desert. So to get water, they live near a river. The river provides water to their farms.

Crops grow in this desert area because the river provides water.

Today as well as long ago, there are many reasons why people live near rivers.

Do you live near a river?

Words You Know

irrigation

New Orleans

New York City

Pittsburgh

port

waterfall

waterwheel

31

Index

About the Author

Allan Fowler is a freelance writer with a background in advertising. Born in New York, he now lives in Chicago and enjoys traveling.

Photo Credits

©: Corbis–Bettmann: 15, 30 top right (Nathan Benn), 12, 31 top (Dean Conger), 11 (Philip Gould), 28 (Judy Griesedieck), 17, 30 bottom right (Charles E. Rotkin), cover (Phil Schermeister), 4, 30 bottom left (Joseph Sohm/Chromo-Sohm Inc.), 8; Landslides Aerial Photography: 27 (Alex S. Maclean); Liaison Agency Inc.: 20, 31 bottom right (Wernher Krutein); Monkmeyer Press: 23 (Conklin); Superstock, Inc.: 7 (Christie's, London), 19, 24, 30 top left, 31 bottom left.

Map by Bob Italiano.